SCHIRMER'S LIBRARY
OF MUSICAL CLASSICS

Vol. 2081

CELLO CLASSICS

19 Pieces by 14 Composers
Intermediate to Advanced Level

For Cello and Piano

ISBN 978-1-4234-2853-4

G. SCHIRMER, Inc.

DISTRIBUTED BY

HAL•LEONARD®
CORPORATION
7777 W. BLUEMOUND RD. P.O. BOX 13819 MILWAUKEE, WI 53213

Visit Hal Leonard Online at
www.halleonard.com

CONTENTS

Sonata No. 1 in B-flat Major

**Solo part edited and
bass realized by
Analee Bacon**

Luigi Boccherini
(1743–1805)

Grave

* in Ms., previous bar repeated in bass by mistake.

Minuetto

(Fine)

* E♭ in Ms.

D.C. fino al 𝄐

Allegro non troppo

first movement from the *Sonata No. 1 in E minor*, Op. 38

**Edited by
Edwin Hughes and
Cornelius van Vliet**

Johannes Brahms
(1833–1897)

Marks of expression in parenthesis are interpretations by the editors.

Copyright, 1921, by G. Schirmer, Inc.

espress. legato

(p)

(mp)

espr.

legato

p

cresc. molto

cresc. molto

ff

ff

Rondo

second movement from the *Sonata in F Major*, Op. 5, No. 1

Ludwig van Beethoven
(1770–1827)

La Bandoline

François Couperin
(1668–1733)

Largo

third movement from the *Sonata in G minor*, Op. 65

Frédéric Chopin
(1810–1849)

Finale: Allegro

fourth movement from the *Sonata in G minor*, Op. 65

Frédéric Chopin
(1810–1849)

50

Rêverie

Claude Debussy
(1862–1918)

Transcribed by Otto Deri

Après un Rêve

Transcribed by Otto Deri

Gabriel Fauré
(1845–1924)

Lento—Allegro maestoso

first movement from the *Concerto in D minor*

Édouard Lalo
(1823–1892)

Edited by
Otto Deri

Sonata No. 4 in G minor

Benedetto Marcello
(1686–1739)

Allegro

Allegro appassionata
Op. 43

Camille Saint-Saëns
(1835–1921)

Allegro appassionato

The Swan

from *Carnival of the Animals*

Camille Saint-Saëns
(1835–1921)

Mélodie
elegy from *The Erynnies*, Op. 10

Jules Massenet
(1842–1912)

Sonata No. 3 in A minor

Antonio Vivaldi
(1678–1741)

Allegro (energico)

Allegro (Allegretto moderato, poco giocondo)

(This page has been intentionally left blank to facilitate page turns.)

Sonata No. 1 in D minor

Solo part edited and
bass realized by
Analee Bacon

Alessandro Scarlatti
(1660–1725)

I

II

Allegretto

III

Largo

IV

A tempo giusto

*Scarlatti has an E here.

Sonata No. 2 in C minor

I

Largo

Alessandro Scarlatti
(1660–1725)

II

Allegretto

III

Largo

IV

Presto

Sonata No. 3 in C Major

I

Alessandro Scarlatti
(1660–1725)

Largo

II

Allegretto

III

Amoroso

Presto

IV